GW01549810

TRINITY GUILDHALL

TRINITY GUILDHALL

TRINITY GUILDHALL